ANIMAL AHa!

THRILLING DISCOVERIES in WILDLIFE SCIENCE

Diane swanson

annick press
toronto + new york + vancouver

Annick Press Ltd.

All rights reserved. No part of this work covered by the copyrights hereon may be reproduced or used in any form or by any means—graphic, electronic, or mechanical—without prior written permission of the publisher.

Edited and copyedited by Elizabeth McLean
Proofread by Helen Godolphin
Cover and interior design by Irvin Cheung / iCheung Design, inc.
Cover illustration by Sean Langedijk
Front cover photographs: camera, istockphoto.com/Jakub Semeniuk; elephant, istockphoto.com/ Clayton Hansen; gorilla, ©Thomas Breuer - MPI-EVA/WCS; python, John Mitchell/First Light; rat, istockphoto.com/Fabian Guignard. Back cover photographs: cockroach, © istockphoto.com/James Steidl; lorikeet, © istockphoto.com/John Austin. Full photo credits on page 47.

We acknowledge the support of the Canada Council for the Arts, the Ontario Arts Council, and the Government of Canada through the Book Publishing Industry Development Program (BPIDP) for our publishing activities.

ONTARIO ARTS COUNCIL
CONSEIL DES ARTS DE L'ONTARIO

Cataloging in Publication

Swanson, Diane, 1944–

    Animal aha! : thrilling discoveries in wildlife science / Diane Swanson.

Includes bibliographical references and index.
ISBN 978-1-55451-164-8 (pbk.).—ISBN 978-1-55451-165-5 (bound)

    1. Animals—Juvenile literature. 2. Animals—Anecdotes—Juvenile literature. 3. Animals—Miscellanea—Juvenile literature. I. Title.
QL49.S899 2009   j590   C2008-905594-2

Printed and bound in China

Published in the U.S.A. by
Annick Press (U.S.) Ltd.

Distributed in Canada by
Firefly Books Ltd.
66 Leek Crescent
Richmond Hill, ON
L4B 1H1

Distributed in the U.S.A. by
Firefly Books (U.S.) Inc.
P.O. Box 1338
Ellicott Station
Buffalo, NY 14205

Visit our website at www.annickpress.com

contents

DiSCOVERiNG THE WONDER OF WiLDLiFE

There's no doubt about it. Scientists work hard to uncover some of the amazing things that animals do. They spend thousands of hours planning experiments, making observations, spotting patterns, and analyzing results. Their efforts call for plenty of patience and loads of persistence. But that all pays off big time when they discover something new—

Even beachcombing naturalists can discover fascinating critters.

Scientists sometimes observe wildlife in their own habitats.

something no one has ever seen before. As you might imagine, finding an AHA! in research is a huge thrill.

Scientists study wildlife as large as whales and as small as insects to learn more about what, how, and why critters do what they do. Some research is done in the wild to see how the animals behave in their natural homes. Other research takes place in laboratories where scientists can watch what happens in controlled experiments. Now and then, a discovery even helps us understand more about people.

This book looks at scientists who have made recent, exciting discoveries about wildlife. Their work has

A mouse is one of the most common subjects used for lab research.

been reported in professional science journals, but not everyone agrees with the results. All research conclusions must be proven by other scientists studying more animals and, perhaps, taking different approaches. Sometimes conclusions change because of new observations.

The stories of the AHA! moments in wildlife science are awesome. One day, they may even inspire you to unravel animal secrets.

GORiLLAS THAT USE TOOLS

The female gorilla had no idea how much excitement she was causing. She was simply wading through a swamp in a dense Congo rainforest. But when the water reached her waist, she stopped suddenly.

Looking around, the gorilla snapped off a thick, leafless branch that was poking out of the water. Then she continued wading, using the sturdy branch to check and recheck the depth of the water. Every now and then, she leaned on the branch for support—as you might if you were hiking across rough ground.

Perched on a platform built high in the treetops, biologist

FAST FACTS

KiNDS: 2 gorilla species
HOME: rainforests of central Africa
FOOD: fruit, flowers, leaves, stems, seeds, insects, and more
SiZE: up to 1.8 meters (6 feet) tall when upright
LifeSpan: about 35 years in the wild

A wading gorilla uses a tool
a stick to check water depth.

Dr. Thomas Breuer and his research team were watching.
Although their telescopes were focused on the female
gorilla, they could scarcely believe their eyes. Never
before had anyone recorded gorillas in the wild using
tools, as captive ones sometimes did. Yet that was exactly
what had just happened.

For a long time, scientists had wondered why no one
had spotted wild gorillas with tools. After all, the animals

had been well studied. Dr. Dian Fossey, for one, had spent years with mountain gorillas in Africa. Famous from the book and movie *Gorillas in the Mist*, she had camped close to the animals and observed them well. But Dr. Fossey had never seen them pick up tools of any kind.

That seemed odd because other great apes often use tools. Chimpanzees break nuts with rocks. Orangutans scoop up food with sticks. And of course, people— who are also great apes—use tools for everything from opening cans of corn to firing rockets into space.

However, gorillas differ from their ape cousins in several ways. Take meat-eating, for example. Chimpanzees sometimes devour monkeys—or even small antelopes—and orangutans occasionally feed on small, monkeylike animals called slow lorises. No one has ever recorded a sighting of gorillas eating flesh, though. Their long, pointed teeth help them rip up plants instead. But gorillas *do eat* a lot. A big male gobbles up to 23 kilograms (50 pounds) a day. That's like you eating 200 bananas every 24 hours!

Gorillas usually rely on their own bodies and strength—not on tools—to get food. They don't need rocks to break open small nuts like chimpanzees do because a gorilla's teeth and jaws are strong enough for the job. And while orangutans use sticks like chisels to break into termite mounds, gorillas just shatter the mounds with their fists. They have massive muscles, especially the males.

So a gorilla checking water depth with a branch was news. Big news. And a month later, when the same researchers spotted another gorilla using a tool, they figured that the big apes might be smarter than people had ever thought. After all, besides making life easier, being able to use tools is an important sign of intelligence.

The second gorilla had been using its tool—the snapped-off stump of a dead bush—in two ways. First, it shoved the stump into the ground, making a firm base for one hand while yanking out water herbs with the other. Next, it laid the stump down flat over squishy mud to form a bridge.

You might think that Dr. Breuer and his team had just been lucky enough to be in the right place at the right time. But their luck had come after 10 years of taking turns observing the gorillas that visited the swampy clearing. While trying to learn more about how these great apes live in the wild, the scientists had spotted at least one group each day.

Impressive muscles ripple across the back of this gorilla.

BRE AK!

A gorilla breaks off a tree to use as a tool.

The gorillas had become used to seeing the team on the platform, and seemed to behave normally.

Finally, all those years of waiting and watching had paid off. Not only did the researchers spy the gorillas using tools, they also took pictures of the action— evidence to show the world.

"This is a truly astounding discovery," said Dr. Breuer. And he thinks that maybe … just maybe … gorillas might teach tool use to other gorillas. More patient watching might show whether or not he's right.

FUN Facts

 Like your fingerprints, a gorilla's nose prints are unique.

Gorillas eat clay. It contains minerals not found in their regular food.

 Gorillas can grab things with their feet because their big toes act like thumbs.

 Every night, gorillas weave branches and leaves into fresh ground nests for sleeping.

Gorillas normally walk on all fours, using their feet and the knuckles on their hands.

ELEPHANTS THAT RECOGNIZE THEIR REFLECTIONS

REFLECTIONS

FAST FACTS

KINDS: 2 elephant species
HOME: grasslands and forests in Africa and Asia
FOOD: grass, leaves, twigs, fruit, and more
SIZE: up to 4 meters (13 feet) tall
LIFESPAN: about 70 years in the wild

Three grown elephants peered into a wide, full-length mirror. It was bolted firmly to the wall inside a New York zoo.

The animals were clearly curious. First, they tried to find out if anything—or anyone—was behind the mirror. They swung their trunks over the wall and even attempted to climb up it. They knelt down and felt beneath the mirror.

What the elephants *didn't* do was ignore their reflection, or treat it as if it were another animal.

"HEY, THAT'S ME!"

this zoo elephant might be thinking.

14

Few animals recognize their own reflection; in fact, until this experiment only great apes—including people—appeared to do that.

Researchers had wondered if elephants might be smart enough to recognize themselves. That's why a team of university scientists, headed by Josh Plotnik, set up an experiment in the New York zoo. What they discovered amazed them.

By feeling all around the mirror, the elephants began to understand that they were seeing their own reflection. To make sure, they appeared to experiment. They moved their heads in and out of view, and waved their long trunks around. They lumbered back and forth. And they observed themselves eating hay in front of the mirror.

The elephants even checked out different parts of their bodies. For example, they poked the tips of their trunks into their mouths. They yanked their big, floppy ears to and fro.

Most intriguing was the elephant that put the tip of her trunk to a white "X" researchers had painted above one of her eyes. In fact, in 90 seconds, the elephant touched that letter 12 times. She likely found the white "X" by seeing it in the mirror. To be certain that the elephant was responding to her image in the mirror and not to what she felt on her skin, the researchers had also painted an invisible, colorless "X" above the other eye. The elephant ignored it completely.

Surprising stuff? Yes, but then, elephants are known to have complex brains, which is why the researchers set out to discover more about their smarts. Scientists already knew that wild elephants are clever enough to guide their herds to the best spots to eat and drink. Elephants can also remember the calls of many other elephants, which helps them identify the ones they meet and know which are friendly. Trainers have taught

An elephant herd has followed the leader to a favorite watering hole.

SLAM DUNK!

A trained elephant scores again.

domesticated elephants to follow about 100 commands, such as "Kneel" and "Turn."

Besides their smarts, elephants are famous for their size. They are the biggest land animals on Earth, and they keep growing as long as they live. When elephants stand on their back legs and stick their trunks in the air, they are tall enough to pluck and munch leaves from trees more than two stories high. Fully grown, an elephant can weigh as much as six small cars stacked together.

Strong elephants help workers in logging camps.

Elephants are as strong as they are big. For thousands of years, people used the great beasts to haul heavy cargo across long distances. In some countries, workers still depend on elephants to move huge logs by pushing, dragging, or picking them up. A large adult can scoop up a 400-kilogram (880-pound) log with its tusks alone.

What the mirror experiment by the research team did was to give the world the first evidence that elephants were intelligent enough to recognize themselves. Earlier experiments hadn't produced the same results, but they had involved small mirrors that failed to reflect the animal's entire body. Elephants would naturally be more familiar with the whole body reflections they see in water, which probably explains why they didn't respond to the smaller mirrors. Besides, they weren't able to reach the little mirrors, so they couldn't check behind or beneath them—as they did with the large mirrors.

Next, scientists might try to discover when elephants *first* begin to recognize their own reflections. After all, that's something you started doing when you were about 18 months old.

STRETCH!
Reach!

An elephant grabs lunch up high.

FUN Facts

Elephant tusks are teeth that grow up to 3 meters (10 feet) long.

To call long distances, elephants make low-pitched sounds that they feel with their feet and hear with their ears.

Dust or mud on an elephant's body helps it avoid sunburn.

One elephant's ear can weigh as much as a slim woman— about 50 kilograms (110 pounds).

The skin of an elephant is about 2.5 centimeters (1 inch) thick.

DOLPHINS tHaT DO (BaSiC MATH)

FAST FACTS

Kinds: more than 30 dolphin species

Home: oceans around the world (some species live in rivers)

Food: fish, squid, shrimp, seals, and more

Size: from 1.5 meters (5 feet) to 9 meters (30 feet) long

Lifespan: possibly up to about 45 years in the wild

A sleek bottlenose dolphin suddenly rose out of the water. With its beaklike snout, it tapped one of two black boards, then slipped back down. SPLASH!

A shrill whistle sounded, and a trainer tossed the dolphin a fish. At the same time, she cheered, clapped her hands, and praised him: "Good boy! All right! I knew you'd get that one."

But when the dolphin tried the same task again, silence

21

followed. No whistle sounded. Nor did the trainer throw any praise or fish his way. The dolphin had failed a math question, but soon returned to try again.

For a long time, scientists had known that dolphins are amazingly smart. They knew, for instance, that these small whales make identifying whistles, and that they can change the length and pitch of these whistles to send other dolphins messages. That could be how they say things such as "Help! I'm over here, and I'm in trouble." Another sign of their intelligence is the ability to play—something only clever animals do. Just for fun, dolphins chase each other,

A dolphin touches the board with fewer dots while the trainer sits inside a shelter.

leap over waves, and flip somersaults. They even tease pelicans by snatching the birds' tail feathers.

But until experiments were held at the Dolphin Research Center in Florida, no one knew that dolphins also had math skills. A research team headed by Dr. Kelly Jaakkola set out to see if the animals could understand some basic math: the difference between less and more. The team wanted to find out exactly what kinds of thinking—including mathematical thinking—dolphins share with humans.

First, the trainers prepared two dolphins for the research. They taught the animals to touch a single black board with white dots on it by rewarding them with fish and praise each time they did. Then the trainers added a second black board and rewarded the dolphins only when they touched the board that had fewer dots on it.

Above or below the ocean's surface, a dolphin can see well.

When the dolphins were ready for testing, a trainer sat inside an open canvas shelter. A black board marked with white dots stood on either side of her. Inside the shelter, the trainer couldn't see the boards, so she couldn't affect the results. The two dolphins taking the tests could see the boards clearly, though. Dolphins have great eyesight in both air and water.

A researcher hid behind the trainer's shelter. After each test, she pulled the boards back and changed the dots. She not only switched the *number* of dots, anywhere between one and eight, but she also used different *sizes* of dots. As well, she set the dots in different *places*. Every time, the dolphins' job was to choose the board with fewer dots.

Whenever one of the animals picked the correct board, the researcher blew her whistle, and the trainer rewarded the dolphin with fish and praise. Again and again, the dolphins were tested. For two weeks, they checked 40 boards a day.

Both dolphins scored well, and they made their choices surprisingly fast—in only a few seconds. One of them chose the correct boards 83 percent of the time. The other earned a score of 82 percent. Their high marks

Standing where the dolphins can't see her, a researcher sets up the testing boards.

couldn't have been due just to luck. The dolphins chose the correct boards much more often than if they had simply guessed.

It may seem odd to think of dolphins doing math. But out at sea, knowing the difference between less and more could be important. For instance, scientists think that it helps dolphins find food. "It would be very useful to keep track of which areas were richer food sources," said Dr. Laela Sayigh of the Woods Hole Oceanographic Institute. University scientist Dr. Stan Kuczaj agrees: "When corralling fish, you might want a good number but not so many that it's overwhelming."

"We are the first in the world to show that dolphins can do this basic math, and yes, I am very proud," said Dr. Jaakkola. Now the research team is hoping to discover even more about the math that dolphins might know and use.

FUN Facts

Dolphins can dive 300 meters (1000 feet) underwater and leap 6 meters (20 feet) into the air.

The high-pitched clicking of dolphins bounces off their prey, helping them find food.

A young dolphin can increase its weight seven times in its first year.

Dolphins have been trained to tail-walk—to walk on their tails at the surface of the water.

Several hundred dolphins might belong to one large group, or pod.

PARROTS THAT SPEAK with MEANING

Scientist Dr. Irene Pepperberg showed a green paper triangle to an African gray parrot. "What's this, Alex?" she asked.

"Paper," answered the parrot.

"What color paper?"

"Green," he said.

"What shape paper?"

"Three-corner."

"Yes! Good!"

Next Dr. Pepperberg held up some keys and asked, "How many?"

"Five," counted Alex. And he was right.

FAST FACTS

KINDS: about 350 parrot species

HOME: forests, grasslands, and deserts in warm areas worldwide

FOOD: seeds, flowers, leaves, fruit, insects, and more

SIZE: 8 centimeters (3 inches) to 1 meter (3 feet) long

LIFESPAN: 15 to 70 years in the wild

Alex was a parrot that seemed to speak with meaning—not just mimicry, or copying. He could name seven colors: rose (red), green, yellow, blue, orange, gray (silver to black), and purple. He could also identify five shapes, saying two-corner for a football shape, three-corner for a triangle, four-corner for a square, five-corner for a pentagon, and six-corner for a hexagon. What's more, he could count items—up to six. Alex could identify a wide range of objects, too. He could

Working for 30 years with Dr. Irene Pepperberg, Alex learned some simple English.

even state which was bigger or smaller, and what was the same or different about two objects. And to do all this, he used human speech.

The parrot used English to tell his trainers what he wanted. For example, Alex called out "want some water" when he was thirsty or yelled "no" when he rejected toys. And like other parrots, he picked up phrases that he heard repeated, such as "I'll see you tomorrow."

In the wild, parrots normally speak to one another in their own way. They make loud, screeching sounds, including "BRAK" or "AAAK." Some of the sounds are warnings or cries for help. But parrots that learn human speech amaze people.

When Dr. Pepperberg first became interested in the way birds think and learn, she began to work with Alex. She named him using letters in the title of her research project: Avian Learning EXperiment.

GReen!

ORanGe!

For 30 years, Dr. Pepperberg taught and studied Alex so she could discover more about the mental abilities of parrots. Alex became famous, appearing on television programs around the world. He was also the subject of many scientific reports.

In her research lab in Massachusetts, Dr. Pepperberg and her trainers used an unusual method to teach Alex to speak English. She let him watch and listen as two people examined and discussed an object—a grape, for example. When one of them named the object correctly, that person received it as a reward. When the person named the object incorrectly, it was taken away. Then the trainers exchanged roles so that Alex could learn

Alex could count the keys AND name their colors.

both parts. The purpose was to make him want to name and receive the object, too. It worked. Next, a trainer helped him say each new word as clearly as possible.

Dr. Pepperberg reports that African gray parrots, such as Alex, are among the smartest birds in the whole parrot family. "They have about the same intelligence as a five-year-old child," she says. "But their communication skills—at least as far as we've looked at in the lab—are only about that of a two-year-old."

Sometimes Alex acted a lot like a two-year-old person might. When he was annoyed, he would nip his trainers and say, "I'm sorry"—then turn around and nip them again!

Still, there's no question that Alex was a bright animal, especially for a bird with a brain the size of a shelled walnut. (Your brain likely weighs about 260 times more than his did.) Before he died in 2007—at age 31—Alex was actually learning to connect letters with sounds, which is what you did when you began to read.

Dr. Pepperberg's research destroyed the idea that parrots only mimic speech. Her work with Alex and the other African gray parrots in her lab has changed the way people imagine "bird brains."

It has even helped children who have problems speaking. In fact, learning to talk the way Dr. Pepperberg's parrots learn helped one boy say his first words—and in complete sentences.

FUN Facts

Like you, a parrot shapes its sounds, in part, by shifting the position of its tongue.

Parrot mates often growl and gurgle as they groom each other.

Some parrots act as lookouts, watching for danger while their flock feeds.

Parrots can hang upside down from branches, even when taking showers in the rain.

Parrot beaks never stop growing. Chewing hard things helps control their size.

PYTHONS that GROW HUGE HEARTS

FAST FACTS

KiNDS: more than 30 python species

HOME: forests, grasslands, swamps, and deserts in Africa, Asia, and Australia

FOOD: birds, lizards, rats, goats, and more

SiZE: 1 meter (3 feet) to 9 meters (30 feet) long

LiFESPAN: up to 20 years in the wild

The Burmese python lay perfectly still inside its cage. Two days earlier, it had stuffed itself with a huge meal of rats. Now it was digesting that dinner, and its body was HARD at work. The python was burning up the same amount of energy as it would if it were moving fast. What's more, it would be using that much energy for many days—as though it were taking part in a long race, not just lying around.

Feeding is a big job for a Burmese python. Unlike you, it can't cut its food into small chunks, then use its teeth to chomp them up. Instead, the snake must grab, hold, and squeeze its prey until the "meal" cannot breathe anymore. Then the python swallows its prey *whole*—fur or feathers, skin, bones, teeth, and all. The snake depends on digestion alone to break down a meal.

And what a feast it is. In a single feeding, the python can easily swallow more than half its weight in food, and it's one of the largest snakes on the planet. A Burmese python weighs as much as a tall man—up to 90 kilograms (200 pounds). No wonder the snake doesn't need to dine often. Six months or more can pass between meals.

After swallowing a rat, a python settles down to digest it.

This big python is swallowing a pig as large as a medium-sized dog.

Scientists had already discovered that a python uses plenty of oxygen when it digests big meals. But to help its blood move that extra oxygen around its long body, the snake needs an especially strong heart—one that has plenty of "pump power."

No one knew *how* it was possible for a Burmese python to gain more of this power. So Dr. James Hicks and his research team decided to find out. In their university lab in California, they studied three groups of Burmese pythons:

- those that had not eaten recently;
- those that had been digesting rats for two days; and
- those that had finished digesting their meals.

As scientists studied each group, they examined the hearts of the pythons. And they found something truly astonishing. Within only two days of feeding, the python hearts put on a lot of muscle. They bulked up big-time. Each of the muscle cells that make up a python's heart enlarged, making the heart itself 40 percent bigger than normal.

Dr. Hicks had never heard of an animal that could change the size of its heart that fast. Just as you'd expect, the larger heart was also much stronger. It was able to pump more oxygen-carrying blood each time it beat.

The researchers discovered that the new, super size of a python's heart lasts up to a week or two after every feeding. Then it starts to shrink. About four weeks after the snake has fed, its heart returns to its usual size.

Open-mouthed, a Burmese python is ready to nab dinner.

Like other snakes, a python sometimes sheds a thin outer layer of skin.

Being able to digest meals by growing a bigger heart very fast is vital to the health of a python. If the snake digested its food slowly, its prey could begin to rot while still inside the snake. That would make the python sick. Even worse, it's possible for gases leaking out of rotting prey to explode.

Like the Burmese python, you are able to grow a bigger heart. But yours would not increase nearly as fast or as much as the snake's heart. Nor could you ever enlarge your heart just by stuffing yourself with food. Instead, you would have to exercise a lot, working out for months.

Still, scientists, including Dr. Hicks, think that studying the hearts of Burmese pythons might help provide clues about how human hearts grow and develop. And one day, those clues might benefit you.

FUN Facts

Large pythons can kill and eat animals as big as deer and leopards.

Some pythons climb trees easily, using their strong tails to hang onto branches.

Unlike most other snakes, a mother python guards her eggs, coiling her long body around them.

Most pythons swim well. Some have traveled 50 kilometers (30 miles) between islands.

An Indian python can stay underwater 30 minutes or more.

COCKROACHES that LEARN at NIGHT

Inside a glass dish, a cockroach fluttered the pair of long antennae on top of its head. The insect sensed some peppermint on the side of the dish. Almost instantly, it charged straight toward the smell. But . . . hold on. The smell of peppermint doesn't normally attract cockroaches. For reasons nobody understands, it even sends them running the other way.

FAST FACTS

KINDS: more than 4,500 cockroach species

HOME: soil, logs, caves, tunnels, and buildings around the world

FOOD: nearly everything—from ink and old clothes to rotting plants and animals

SIZE: from 2.5 millimeters (1/10 inch) to 10 centimeters (4 inches) long

LIFESPAN: up to 2 years in the wild

Dr. Terry Page holds one of the cockroaches from the experiments.

But this was no ordinary cockroach. It had been to university where it had *learned* to like the smell of peppermint. Its lessons were part of experiments that scientists were doing to discover the times of day when some animals might learn best.

Dr. Terry Page and his research team had decided to use cockroaches instead of other common lab animals, such as mice, because—for one thing—cockroaches don't bite! The researchers chose a cockroach species (*Leucophaea maderae)* that had been used in many biology experiments, so a lot was known about it—even though it doesn't usually live around people.

The cockroaches also made good subjects for these learning experiments because they had already proven they *could* be taught. Over the years, they had done some amazing feats, such as finding their way through complex mazes.

For two years, the research team took hundreds of cockroaches to school. In a university lab in Tennessee, they trained the insects to link the smell of peppermint with tasty sugar water. The cockroaches also learned to link the smell of vanilla—which they normally like— with something they don't care for: salty water.

In training the cockroaches, the researchers put each insect into a small plastic tube. They soaked a teeny bit of paper with peppermint extract and held it between the insect's antennae, just above its head. Four seconds later—after the insect had smelled the paper—they placed a drop of sugar water on its mouthparts.

In the same way, the team gave the same insect some vanilla-soaked paper to smell and followed up with a drop of salty water. Because the researchers wanted to find out the times of day when cockroaches learn best, they trained some of the insects in the morning and others at night.

Then came the tests. The team set each roach down in the middle of a large, round dish. Along the edge were drops of peppermint and vanilla extracts in small dishes. If you can picture the bowl as a clock face, the extracts were placed at numbers 3, 6, 9, and 12. The researchers watched which odor the cockroach headed toward. Once it found the smell, the extract dishes were moved around randomly, and the cockroach was tested again and again—for 10 minutes.

The researchers tested the memory of every cockroach, one by one.

Some cockroaches were tested 30 minutes after training, checking short-term memory. Others were tested 48 hours later, checking long-term memory.

How did they perform? The cockroaches that were trained at night remembered equally well at night or in the morning. What's more, they remembered what they'd learned for at least 48 hours. The cockroaches that were trained in the morning scored far worse. They couldn't remember at any time of day. One group was tested only 5 minutes after training and couldn't recall what it had learned.

"They forgot everything and behaved as if they had no training at all," said Dr. Page, but he has no idea why that's so. Perhaps more research will reveal the answer. Still, he thinks that experiments like this point to strong links between learning, memory, and biological clocks—the times when animals are more or less alert.

"This is the first example of an insect whose ability to learn is controlled by its biological clock," he added proudly. What he and his team discovered might also apply to other animals. Even your learning might be affected by your biological clock. And just think, if you don't "do" mornings, you can always look to cockroaches for company.

FUN Facts

Cockroaches have lived on Earth—unchanged—for about 400 million years.

Many female cockroach species lay eggs, but some give birth to live young.

A headless cockroach can walk around for a while, and its detached head can wave its antennae.

Brown-banded cockroaches, called TV cockroaches, often crawl inside televisions to warm up.

Madagascar hissing cockroaches are loud enough to frighten dogs.

inDex

acknowledgments

Besides ever-vigilant editor Elizabeth McLean, ingenious designer Irvin Cheung and the whole gang at Annick Press, I want to thank the scientists who kindly reviewed each of the chapters in my manuscript and helped to provide the photographs: Dr. Thomas Breuer, Dr. James Hicks, Dr. Kelly Jaakkola, Dr. Terry Page, Dr. Irene Pepperberg, and Josh Plotnik. Their research in animal science is impressive!

As well, I acknowledge the insight I received from the writings of many scientists, science journalists, and institutes, in particular David Adam, "Captured on film: wild gorilla using a walking stick," *The Guardian*; Rachel Adelson, "Marine mammals master math," *Science Watch*; The Alex Foundation; Johnnie B. Andersen, Bryan C. Rourke, Vincent J. Caiozzo, Albert F. Bennett and James W. Hicks, "Physiology: Postprandial cardiac hypertrophy in pythons," *Nature*; BBC News; Thomas Breuer, Mireille Ndoundou-Hockemba, Vicki Fishlock, "First Observation of Tool Use in Wild Gorillas," *PLoS: Biology*; The British Library (online); Chris Bryant, "Python Research Gives Insight into Digestion," *University of Alabama Research Magazine*; Benedict Careyer, "A thinking parrot's loving good-bye," *International Herald Tribune*; Charles Choi, "Elephant Self-Awareness Mirrors Humans," *LiveScience*; Philip Cohen, "Humans and Parrots May Share Sharp Tongues," NewScientist.com; Susan Decker, Shannon McConnaughey, and Terry L. Page, "Circadian regulation of insect olfactory learning," *Proceedings of the National Academy of Sciences*; Discovery Channel; Dolphin Discovery Centre, Western Australia; Dolphin Research Center; Richard Farinato, "Parrots," Florida Museum of Natural History; Henry Fountain, "The Heart of a Snake (and That's Good)," *New York Times*; Birute Galdikas, *Great Ape Odyssey*; Belinda Goldsmith, "Don't bug them! Cockroaches don't like mornings," Reuters; The Gorilla Foundation; The Humane Society of the USA; Indianapolis Zoological Society; Kelly Jaakkola, Wendi Fellner, Linda Erb, Mandy Rodriguez, Emily Guarino, "Understanding of the concept of numerically less by bottlenose dolphins," *Journal of Comparative Psychology*; Peter Jackson, *Endangered Species: Elephants*; Eric Jaffe, "Mirror Image," Smithsonian.com; Elizabeth Pennisi Juengst, "Elephant Matriarchs Tell Friend from Foe," *Science*; Robin Lloyd, "The Truth about Cockroaches," *LiveScience*; Marine Mammal Center, California; S. Milius, "Friend or Foe? Old Elephants Know," *Science News*; Susan Milius, "Shortcut to a Big Heart," *Science News*; Steve Nadis, "Who You Calling Dumbo? Researchers Test the Elephant's Mighty Memory," *Omni*;

National Geographic News; National Parks, New South Wales, Australia; National Primate Research Center, University of Wisconsin-Madison; National Science Foundation; Newsinfo, Indiana University; Newswise; Tuan C. Nguyen, "Cockroaches Are Not Morning People," *LiveScience*; ParrotChronicles.com; John Roach, "Elephants Recognize Selves in Mirror, Study Says," *National Geographic News*; John Roach, "Vibrations," *National Geographic News*; John Roach, "Wild Gorillas Use Tools, Photos Reveal," *National Geographic News*; David F. Salisbury, "The cockroach's ability to learn varies dramatically with the time of day," *Exploration*; Russell Smith with Dr. Irene Pepperberg, CBC Radio; John Stidworthy, *Snakes of the World*; Lester Swan and Charles Papp, *The Common Insects of North America*; Ron Toft, "Delightful Bottlenose Dolphins," *Ahlan Wasahlan*; tursiops.org; Kirsten Veness, "Parrots 'as intelligent' as young children," *The World Today*; Jennifer Viegas, *Discovery News*; Western Illinois University; World Wildlife Fund, United Kingdom.

PHOTO CREDITS

All photographs are the copyright of the photographers, reprinted with permission. i lorikeet, © istockphoto.com/John Austin; camera, © istockphoto.com/Jakub Semeniuk; python, © Bryan Rourke; 4 naturalist and horseshoe crab, © istockphoto.com; 5 scientist and penguin, © istockphoto.com/André Schäfer; 6 lab rat, © istockphoto.com; 8 gorilla, © Thomas Breuer - MPI-EVA/WCS; 10 gorilla back, © istockphoto.com; 11 gorilla and stick, © Thomas Breuer - MPI-EVA/WCS; 12 gorilla face © istockphoto.com/Eric Isselée; gorilla foot, © istockphoto.com/Steffen Foerster; 14 elephant and mirror, taken from Plotnik J., Reiss D., de Waal, FBM. 2006. "Self-recognition in an Asian elephant." Proceedings of the National Academy of Sciences USA 103:17053–57; 16 elephants at water hole, © istockphoto.com/Nico Smit; 17 elephant playing basketball, © istockphoto.com/Volker Gaudl; 18 elephants logging, © istockphoto.com; 19 elephant stretching, © istockphoto.com/Lorenzo Pastore; 20 elephant in dust, © istockphoto.com/ Karel Gallas; 22 dolphin and trainer © Dolphin Research Center www.dolphins.org; 23 dolphin portrait © Javier Gutierrez/First Light; 24 researcher sets up testing boards © Dolphin

about the author

Diane Swanson, a self-professed "nature nut," is noted
for unearthing fascinating, kid-friendly facts about
science and nature. She is the award-winning author of
over 70 books for children and more than 450 magazine
articles.

Swanson was the recipient of the prestigious Orbis Pictus
Award for Outstanding Nonfiction for Children, as
well as the International Youth Library's White Raven
Award. Her books have appeared on numerous "best of"
recommended lists for children. She lives in Victoria, BC.